THE Foodie TRIVIA BOOK

By Jenine Zimmers

Copyright ©2023

Welcome to "The Foodie Trivia Book," a collection of food and drink trivia questions to determine if you can truly call yourself a foodie! Questions come in groups of five, and are divided by country, region, and food type. You'll be tested on the origins of iconic dishes, quirky food customs, and specific ingredients from around the globe.

To play for points, divide into two teams. Teams take turns tackling a food category, each of which contains five questions. One point is awarded for each correct answer. Alternate reading and answering questions for each category. You may play the whole book in one game, or stop at page 46 to play half. The team with the most points at the end wins!

You may also test yourself by moving through the book solo. As a bonus, fun facts are sprinkled throughout the pages for your enjoyment.

No matter the method you choose, this book will tantalize your taste buds and leave you hungry for more!

Bon Appétit!

CONTENTS

Italian Food

1. What is the main ingredient in gnocchi?

2. Amaretti are crunchy biscuits made with which nut?

3. What Italian liqueur is typically served as an after-dinner digestive?

4. Arborio Rice is typically used in which Italian dish?

5. What is cannoli filled with?

1. Potato
2. Almond
3. Limoncello
4. Risotto
5. Ricotta

FUN FACT

On Easter Sunday, lamb is traditionally served throughout Italy.

Soul Food

1. Hoppin' John is black-eyed peas served with what?

2. What are grits made from?

3. Black-eyed peas and what other vegetable are eaten for luck on New Year's Day?

4. What bread is traditionally served with soul food?

5. What is the official dish of Louisiana?

1. Rice
2. Ground corn
3. Collard greens
4. Cornbread
5. Gumbo

FUN FACT

The term "soul food" was first heard
in African American communities in the 1950s,
and became popular in the 1960s.

French Food

1. What type of meat is used in a Coq au Vin?

2. If you add an egg on top of a Croque Monsieur, what does it become?

3. Bouillabaisse is made using what protein?

4. What is the purpose of a roux in French cooking?

5. What color is Béchamel sauce in French cooking?

1. Chicken
2. Croque Madame
3. Fish
4. To thicken
5. White

FUN FACT

A yellow onion is traditionally used in French onion soup.

Vegetables

1. Americans call it an eggplant, and Brits call it what?

2. What vegetable is said to "grow eyes" as it ages?

3. Which country grows the most asparagus in the world?

4. Which vegetable is the main ingredient of sauerkraut?

5. What do Brussels sprouts contain that causes them to smell?

1. Aubergine
2. Potato
3. China
4. Cabbage
5. Sulfur

FUN FACT

Okra is known as "lady fingers"
in some parts of the world.

Ice Cream

1. When you add ice cream on top of pie, what do you have?

2. What is the most popular ice cream flavor in America?

3. What country is credited with inventing ice cream?

4. First Lady Dolley Madison was said to have invented what ice cream flavor?

5. Ben & Jerry's was founded in which U.S. state?

1. Pie à la mode
2. Vanilla
3. China
4. Strawberry
5. Vermont

FUN FACT

Burton Baskin's name comes first in the Baskin-Robbins brand because he won a coin toss.

Mexican Food

1. What kind of meat is in tacos al pastor?

2. The main ingredient in pozole, a Mexican stew, is hominy, which is made from what vegetable?

3. What Mexican food name translates to "little donkey"?

4. What spicy brown sauce made from many ingredients, including chile, bread crumbs, and chocolate?

5. What Mexican sweet treat is deep-fried pastry stick rolled in sugar?

ANSWERS

1. Pork
2. Corn
3. Burrito
4. Mole
5. Churro

FUN FACT

Guacamole is typically served in a small stone dish called molcajete.

Cheese

1. Which animal's milk is used to make cheddar cheese?

2. What country does Manchego cheese come from?

3. What is the French word for cheese?

4. What are the holes in Swiss cheese called?

5. Which cheese means "recooked" in Italian?

1. Cow
2. Spain
3. Fromage
4. The eyes
5. Ricotta

FUN FACT

Cheese is good for your teeth because it's high in calcium.

Greek Food

1 What vegetable is the main ingredient of melitzanosalata?

2 What ingredient is used as the base for tzatziki dip?

3 What green vegetable is the filling for Spanakopita?

4 What is the most common herb in Greek cooking?

5 Pastitsio is the Greek version of what hearty pasta dish?

ANSWERS

1. Eggplant (or Aubergine)
2. Yogurt
3. Spinach
4. Oregano
5. Lasagna

FUN FACT

Greek legend says the olive tree was a sacred gift from goddess Athena.

Tacos

1. Instead of Taco Tuesday, Norway celebrates tacos on this day.

2. What streaming service offers a taco documentary called "Taco Chronicles"?

3. In what country did hard shell tacos originate?

4. True or false: Americans eat 2.5 billion tacos a year.

5. True or false: When Taco Bell opened in 1962, tacos cost 30 cents each.

1 Friday

2 Netflix

3 United States

4 False: They eat 4.5 billion.

5 False. Each cost 19 cents.

FUN FACT

The Grand Velas Los Cabos resort
in Mexico creates the world's most
expensive taco at $25,000.

Sushi

1. Makizushi is the official name of what type of sushi?

2. True or false: Sushi began as a street food.

3. When fish is placed directly on top of a piece of rice, what type of sushi is it?

4. What is a prime ingredient in an Unagi Roll?

5. Nyotaimori is the art of eating sushi off of what?

ANSWERS

1. Rolled sushi

2. True!

3. Nigiri

4. Eel

5. A person's body

FUN FACT

Pickled ginger is dyed
with beet juice to look pink.

Chocolate

1. What country consumes the most chocolate?

2. What plant is chocolate made from?

3. What chocolate drink did Yankees manager Yogi Berra endorse in the 1950s?

4. A Hershey's Kiss mixed with white chocolate is called?

5. What candy company produced the first box of Valentine's chocolate?

1. Switzerland
2. Cacao Tree
3. Yoo-Hoo
4. A Hug
5. Cadbury

FUN FACT

Nutella was invented in Italy.

Chinese Food

1 What nut is used in Kung Pao Chicken?

2 What is the term for small bite-sized dishes typically served in baskets or on small plates?

3 Congee is a Chinese porridge made by boiling what for a long time?

4 What kitchen item translates to "cooking pot" in Cantonese?

5 What Chinese dish has pork with various vegetables wrapped in a pancake?

1 Peanut

2 Dim sum

3 Rice

4 Wox

5 Moo Shu Pork (or Mu Shu)

FUN FACT

Elders sit and eat first
in Chinese tradition.

Barbecue

1. What is the main ingredient in an Eastern Carolina barbecue sauce?

2. White barbecue sauce is popular in what U.S. state?

3. True or false: McDonald's restaurant started as McDonald's Bar-B-Q.

4. The American Royal World Series of Barbecue takes place in with city?

5. Burnt ends come from what type of meat?

1 Vinegar

2 Alabama

3 True!

4 Kansas City

5 Brisket

FUN FACT

In 1927, Louis Armstrong made his first recording of the iconic tune "Struttin' with Some Barbecue."

 Bread

1. When baking bread, what ingredient causes dough to rise?

2. Germany is known for what dark and heavy rye bread?

3. What bread item is boiled before it's baked for a unique texture?

4. Eggs Benedict is served with what kind of bread?

5. Damper is a traditional soda bread from what country?

1. Yeast

2. Pumpernickel

3. Bagels

4. English muffin

5. Australia

FUN FACT

Sliced bread was invented
in 1928.

Donuts

1. What was the first company to mass-produce donuts?

2. What type of icing is used on Boston cream donuts?

3. For what holiday are jelly doughnuts a traditional food?

4. When is a donut called a beignet?

5. Spudnuts are donuts made with what ingredient in place of flour?

1. Krispy Kreme

2. Chocolate

3. Hanukkah

4. When it has no hole

5. Potato

FUN FACT

In France, Pets de Nonnes, or small donuts, translates to "nun's farts."

Spanish Food

1. What is the name for small plates, snacks, or appetizers served in Spain?

___

2. Which spice gives paella its golden color?

___

3. What type of food is jamón?

___

4. How are croquetas cooked?

___

5. True or false: Seafood is the main protein in Valencian paella.

1 Tapas

2 Saffron

3 Ham

4 Deep-fried

5 False! There is no seafood in Valencian paella.

FUN FACT

Turrón is a popular Spanish dessert served during Christmas.

1. What Italian city is considered the birthplace of pizza?

2. The first pizzeria in the United States was located in what city?

3. What condiment can be found on pizza in Japan?

4. What is the most popular pizza topping in India?

5. What is the most popular pizza topping in the United States?

1. Naples

2. New York City (Lombardi's)

3. Mayonnaise

4. Tofu

5. Pepperoni

FUN FACT

There are about 26,000 books about pizza available on Amazon.

Vietnamese Food

1. Nuac mam is what type of sauce?

2. Bánh Mi is a type of what?

3. Chè refers to several foods in Vietnamese culture that are what in flavor?

4. Gỏi Gá is a crunchy Vietnamese salad featuring what protein?

5. True or false: Vietnam is known for the spiciest curries worldwide.

1. Fish sauce

2. Sandwich

3. Sweet

4. Chicken

5. False! Vietnamese curries are on the milder side.

FUN FACT

Vietnamese food uses little oil or dairy.

Coffee

1. A cup of drip coffee with a shot of espresso added is called what?

2. What is the common name for the coffee brewing device also known as a "plunger pot"?

3. On what sitcom did the coffee shop Central Perk appear?

4. What chocolate-flavored coffee drink gets its name from a city in Yemen?

5. What liquor do you add to coffee to make a Coffee Alexander?

1. Redeye
2. French Press
3. "Friends"
4. Mocha
5. Brandy

FUN FACT

Ludwig van Beethoven was an obsessive coffee fan.

Portuguese Food

1 What type of fish is Bacalhau, which is Portugal's national dish?

---

2 What type of nut is Castanhas, which are popular in Portugal?

---

3 Caldo Verde and Canja de Galinhja are types of what?

---

4 What is the main seafood in Polvo a Lagareiro?

---

5 True or false: Tremoços, or lupini beans, are commonly eaten for dessert in Portugal.

1. Codfish

2. Chestnuts

3. Soup

4. Octopus

5. False! Tremoços is a salty snack served at a bar.

FUN FACT

Portugal imports most of its Bacalhau from Norway.

Fast Food

1. Known for its square hamburgers, which fast food chain is the oldest?

2. What popular fast food item was initially invented as a meat substitute during Lent?

3. How many herbs and spices make up the secret blend used in Kentucky Fried Chicken?

4. What fast food chain uses "Eat Fresh" as its slogan?

5. What chain popularized pizza delivery in the United States?

ANSWERS

1. White Castle
2. Filet-O-Fish (McDonald's)
3. 11
4. Subway
5. Domino's

FUN FACT

Dave Thomas named the Wendy's fast food chain after his daughter.

Fruits

1 What fruit is bought most often
in the United States?

---

2 True or false: A watermelon
is more than 90 percent water.

---

3 What is the only fruit to have
its seeds on the outside?

---

4 What continent are pineapples
originally from?

---

5 India contributes 50 percent
of the global supply of what fruit?

1. Banana

2. True!

3. Strawberry

4. South America

5. Mango

FUN FACT

There are about 2,500 variations of apple grown in the United States.

Wine

1 What is the most widely planted grape in the world?

2 What varietal is Australia's biggest export?

3 What does it mean if a wine is described as "hot"?

4 What country is the world's leading cork producer?

5 Which country has the largest area of vineyards?

1. Cabernet sauvignon

2. Shiraz

3. High in alcohol content

4. Portugal

5. Spain

FUN FACT

Wine is 80-90 percent water.

Caribbean Food

1. Cou-cou and flying fish is the national dish of what country?

2. What Caribbean country is sometimes called the Island of Spice?

3. Mannish Water is a traditional Jamaican soup featuring what protein?

4. Callaloo is a type of what used in popular dishes in many Caribbean countries?

5. In Caribbean rice and peas, the peas are actually what?

1 Barbados

2 Grenada

3 Goat

4 Plant (or vegetable)

5 Beans (Red or kidney)

FUN FACT

Coquito, meaning "Little Coconut,"
is a drink that originated in Puerto Rico that is
typically served for Christmas.

Middle Eastern

1. "Baba Ghannouj" translates to mashed what?

2. Tahini is made by grounding what?

3. What is the deep-fried ball or fritter featured in Middle Eastern cuisine called?

4. Tabbouleh is a cold salad that originated in what country?

5. Mansaf, a traditional Jordanian dish, features what meat served with fermented dried yogurt?

1. Eggplant
2. Sesame seeds
3. Falafel
4. Lebanon
5. Lamb

FUN FACT

Camel meat is popular in some parts
of the Middle East.

Bacon

1. The name bacon refers to what part of the pig?

2. True or false: Scientists have found that bacon can be as addictive as some drugs.

3. A danger dog, which is a hot dog wrapped in bacon and deep-fried, was first sold in what country?

4. In which U.S. city can you find the United Church of Bacon, where people actually worship bacon?

5. In what year was the bacon cheeseburger invented: 1923, 1943, or 1963?

1. The back
2. True!
3. Mexico
4. Las Vegas
5. 1963

FUN FACT

The average American eats 18 pounds
of bacon each year.

Brazilian Food

1 Paçoca is a Brazilian candy made from what nut?

---

2 Coxinha is a Brazilian croquette made using what meat?

---

3 Farofa is small pieces of bacon fried with what flour, which is popular in Brazil?

---

4 Cachaça, Brazil's national liquor, is distilled from what sweet plant?

---

5 Brazil is the world's biggest producer of what fruit?

1. Peanut
2. Chicken
3. Cassava
4. Sugercane
5. Oranges

FUN FACT

Brazilians sometimes use sweet pizza toppings, like banana slices and cinnamon.

French fries

1. Disco fries are made with melted cheese and what other ingredient?

2. What fries are made by pressing batter into a mold?

3. What former president introduced French fries to America?

4. Which type of potato is most commonly used to make French fries?

5. What country, known for its French fries, is home to the Frietmuseum, or French Fry Museum?

ANSWERS

1. Gravy
2. Waffle fries
3. Thomas Jefferson
4. Idaho, or russet
5. Belgium

FUN FACT

Burger King changed its French fry recipe in 2011 to make them thicker and crunchier.

German Food

1. What kind of fish is used to create the iconic German favorite rollmops?

2. Gebrannte mandeln are nuts covered in what?

3. A Kartoffelkloesse is a dumpling made from what vegetable?

4. What fruit is in Germany's famous black forest cake?

5. Stollen is the traditional German fruitcake eaten during what holiday?

1. Herring
2. Sugar
3. Potato
4. Cherry
5. Christmas

To order one beer in Germany,
you should hold up your thumb.

Steaks

1. Tenderloin is known by what other name?

2. "Marbling" is the presence of what in steak?

3. The delicacy of Kobe beef originated in what country?

4. True or false: A porterhouse steak is also called a "T-bone."

5. What well-known steakhouse in Brooklyn was named after its German founder?

1. Filet mignon

2. Fat

3. Japan

4. True

5. Peter Luger Steakhouse

FUN FACT

Japanese Wagyu was named world's best steak at the 2022 World Steak Challenge.

Thai Food

1. What fruit is the main ingredient in Som Tam, a popular Thai salad?

2. Which ingredient is not found in traditional Pad Thai: bean sprouts, tomato, or fried egg?

3. What ingredient gives yellow curry its color?

4. Pad Kra Pao Moo is usually topped with what fried ingredient?

5. True or false: Food in Thailand is almost always eaten with chopsticks.

1. Papaya

2. Tomato

3. Turmeric

4. Egg

5. False! Chopsticks are not a common Thai utensil.

FUN FACT

An oven is rarely used in Thai cooking.

Beer

1 When found on a beer bottle, what does the acronym IPA stand for?

2 Which beer style is known for its dark color and roasted, coffee-like flavor?

3 What is the name of the beer style that originated in Cologne, Germany?

4 What country has the greatest number of beer brands?

5 What is the name for the foam that forms on top of beer?

1. Indian Pale Ale

2. Stout

3. Kölsch

4. Belgium

5. Head

FUN FACT

Portland, Oregon, is nicknamed Beervana because it has so many breweries.

Indian Food

<ol>
<li>What Indian chicken dish is named for the clay oven it's cooked in?</li>
<li>What M word that means "mixture of spices" is often found on Indian menus?</li>
<li>What small puff pastry filled with vegetables or meat is served as an appetizer?</li>
<li>Which of the following is not an Indian bread: Jalfrezi, Naan, or Paratha?</li>
<li>Which Indian curry is the most spicy: Korma, Tikka Masala, or Phaal?</li>
</ol>

1. Tandoori
2. Masala
3. Samosa
4. Jalfrezi
5. Phaal

FUN FACT

Yogurt mixed with honey was known as "food of the gods" in ancient India.

Hot dogs

1. What is the most popular hot dog topping in the United States?

2. What kind of bun is a traditional Chicago hot dog served on?

3. What brand sold the most hot dogs in the United States in 2022?

4. What type of meat do the majority of Americans prefer their hot dogs be made from?

5. What well-known hot dog stand opened in Coney Island in 1916?

1. Mustard
2. Poppy seed bun
3. Ball Park
4. Beef
5. Nathan's Famous

FUN FACT

Hot dogs started selling at baseball games in the early 1890s.

1. What green tea powder is used in traditional Japanese tea ceremonies?

2. What is the name of the process of soaking tea leaves in water to extract the flavor?

3. What are the tapioca pearls in Bubble Tea more commonly known as?

4. Tea is the second most consumed beverage on earth. What's the first?

5. What is the Hindi word for tea?

1 Matcha

2 Steeping

3 Boba

4 Water

5 Chai

FUN FACT

Iced Tea was officially launched at the 1904 World's Fair in St. Louis, Missouri.

Grilled Cheese

1 In what U.S. city is the award-winning restaurant The American Grilled Cheese Kitchen?

2 True or false: The earliest grilled cheese sandwich was made without a top slice of bread.

3 The Elvis Grilled Cheese adds bacon, banana, and what to a traditional grilled cheese?

4 Chef Gordon Ramsey's Ultimate Grilled Cheese Sandwich includes what Korean ingredient?

5 UberEATS found that which day of the week is most popular to order grilled cheese?

1. San Francisco
2. True!
3. Peanut butter
4. Kimchi
5. Saturday

FUN FACT

Diana Duyser sold a grilled cheese sandwich for $28,000 in 2004 because the bread featured an image of the Virgin Mary.

Polish Food

1. Paska is traditionally served on what holiday in Poland?

2. Mizeria is a salad made with sour cream dressing and what vegetable?

3. Polish half moon-shaped dumplings are called what?

4. Golabki is made by stuffing what vegetable?

5. Traditional borscht is a soup made colorful from what vegetable?

1 Easter

2 Cucumber

3 Pierogi

4 Cabbage

5 Beet

FUN FACT

The Pittsburgh Pirates hold a pierogi race during the fifth inning of every game.

Pies

1 What is the star ingredient of a shoofly pie?

---

2 Pie a la mode is pie served with what?

---

3 What is the official state pie of Florida?

---

4 What kind of pie crust is topped with weaved dough strips?

---

5 What type of meat is in a shepherd's pie?

1. Molasses
2. Ice cream
3. Key lime pie
4. Lattice
5. Beef

FUN FACT

New Mexico has a town called Pie Town.

Cheeseburgers

1. Where does the cheese go in a Jucy Lucy burger?

2. In 2005, the Heart Attack Grill made the Quadruple Bypass Burger, which has how many cheese slices?

3. In 1937, Bob's Big Boy became the first restaurant to serve what type of cheeseburger?

4. What kind of cheese is on a McDonald's Big Mac?

5. Chef Bobby Flay's signature "crunch" cheeseburger gets its name from what ingredient?

1 Inside the meat patty

2 Eight

3 Double cheeseburger

4 American

5 Potato chips

FUN FACT

In 2023, Donald Gorske of Wisconsin set the record for eating the most Big Macs in a lifetime with 33,400.

Cocktails

1. A White Russian combines vodka, milk and what?

2. What drink do peach schnapps and orange juice make?

3. What drink is often served in a copper mug?

4. What classic cocktail consists of gin, lime juice, and simple syrup?

5. What ingredient is used to achieve the frothy top in a Pisco Sour?

1. Kahlua
2. Fuzzy navel
3. Moscow mule
4. Gimlet
5. Egg whites

FUN FACT

Jack Daniel's is produced in a dry county in Tennessee, and can't be sold where it's made.

Thank you!

The purchase of this book supported
a small business. We hope you enjoyed it!